Rise from the Pain

A Guide to Rebuilding Your Life After a Painful Breakup

By

Jorvian Maithe

Chapter One

The Initial Shock

At the end of a relationship, you can feel like the rug has been pulled out from under you, leaving you disoriented, heartbroken, and grappling with a whirlwind of emotions. The initial shock of a breakup is often the most challenging phase to navigate. It is a time of raw, unfiltered emotion, where the world as you know it shifts dramatically, and you're left to pick up the pieces. Understanding and acknowledging the profound impact this phase can have on your mental and emotional well-being is crucial for your healing journey.

When a relationship ends, it's not just the loss of a partner but the dissolution of a shared future, a collection of dreams, and an intertwined life. The immediate impact can be overwhelming. You might find yourself questioning everything: your self-worth, your decisions, and the very fabric of your reality. The dreams you built together shatter, leaving a void that feels impossible to fill. This period is often characterized by a profound sense of loss, akin to mourning a loved one's death. The pain is real, palpable, and can manifest in various ways, both emotionally and physically. In the immediate aftermath, grief is a natural and common reaction. It's essential to recognize that grief is not just reserved for death but can be experienced in any significant loss. You might find yourself crying uncontrollably, feeling a deep, aching sadness that permeates every aspect of your life. This grief can be all-consuming, making it difficult to perform even the simplest tasks. It's important to allow yourself to grieve. Suppressing these feelings can prolong your pain and hinder your healing process. Embrace the tears and the sorrow; they are a testament to the love and effort you invested in the relationship.

Anger is another powerful emotion that often accompanies the initial shock of a breakup. You might feel furious at your ex-partner, at yourself, or at the circumstances that led to the end of the relationship. This anger can be intense and overwhelming, making it difficult to think clearly or act rationally. It's a natural response to feeling hurt and betrayed. However, it's crucial to channel this anger constructively. Allow yourself to feel it, but avoid letting it dictate your actions. Engage in physical activities, journal your thoughts, or talk to a trusted friend or therapist to process your anger healthily.

Confusion is an everyday companion to grief and anger during this phase. The abrupt change can leave you questioning everything. You might replay the relationship in your mind, searching for clues and answers. What went wrong? Could you have done something differently? This relentless analysis can be exhausting and often leads to more confusion rather than clarity. It's essential to recognize that some questions may never have satisfying answers. Accepting this uncertainty is a significant step towards healing. Understand that the end of a relationship is rarely a result of a single event or mistake but rather a complex interplay of factors. The emotional turmoil of a breakup can also manifest physically. You might experience symptoms such as insomnia, changes in appetite, fatigue, or even physical pain. These physical reactions are your body's way of coping with the intense emotional stress. It's essential to be kind to yourself during this time. Prioritize self-care, even if it feels like the last thing you want to do. Rest, eat nourishing foods, and engage in gentle physical activity. These small acts of self-care can help your body manage the stress and begin the healing process.

One of the most challenging aspects of the initial shock is the loneliness that often accompanies it. The person you once confided in and shared your daily life with is no longer there. This void can feel immense and all-encompassing. You might feel isolated as if no one truly understands what you're going through. It's crucial to reach out to your support network during this time. Friends and family can provide a listening ear, comfort, and practical help. Don't be afraid to lean on them; they care about you and want to support you. Allowing yourself to feel these emotions entirely is a vital part of the healing process. It's tempting to push the pain away, to distract yourself with work, hobbies, or new relationships. While these strategies might provide temporary relief, they often delay the necessary emotional processing. Embrace your feelings, no matter how uncomfortable they might be. Cry when you need to, scream into a pillow if it helps, and take time to reflect. These emotions are a natural response to loss and an integral part of your journey towards healing.

Remember that it's acceptable to not have everything sorted out while you go through this difficult period. Healing is not a linear process; there will be good and bad days. Some days, the grief may be excruciating, while others, you may see glimmers of hope and strength. Be patient with yourself. Allow yourself to recover at your own speed. There is no set schedule for healing, and comparing your progress to others can be harmful. During this initial phase, it's also essential to establish healthy boundaries with your ex-partner. Whether the breakup was amicable or contentious, taking time apart is crucial. Constant communication can hinder your healing and prolong the emotional rollercoaster. Give yourself the space to gain perspective and begin the process of moving forward. This might mean unfollowing them on social media, avoiding places you frequented together, and resisting the urge to check in on them. It's not about being spiteful but about protecting your emotional well-being. In the throes of the initial shock, it's easy to lose sight of the future. The pain can be so overwhelming that it feels like it will never end. But know that this phase is temporary. As intense as the emotions are, they will eventually subside. With time, the rawness will fade, and you will begin to see glimmers of hope and new possibilities. Healing is a journey, and this initial shock, while profoundly painful, is the first step towards a new beginning.

Throughout this process, self-compassion is paramount. Be gentle with yourself as you navigate the storm of emotions. Acknowledge your pain and validate your feelings. Remind yourself that it's okay to feel this way, that it's a natural response to a significant loss. Practice self-kindness, whether through positive self-talk, mindfulness, or engaging in activities that bring you joy and peace.

The first shock of a breakup is, in the end, a very personal and life-changing event. It is a moment of deep emotion and vulnerability, as well as significant personal growth and discovery. Allowing oneself to feel and process these emotions creates the basis for healing and rebuilding. Accept the trip with an open heart, understanding that every step, no matter how painful, leads to a stronger, more resilient self.

Chapter Two

Understanding the Breakup

After the initial shock of a breakup begins to subside, a natural next step in the healing process is to seek understanding. The desire to make sense of what went wrong, to find reasons and assign meaning to the end of the relationship, is a crucial part of the journey. This phase, though challenging, can be profoundly enlightening and empowering as it encourages introspection and growth. Understanding the breakup involves a thorough examination of both the relationship and yourself, leading to insights that can shape your future interactions and personal development.

Analyzing the reasons behind a breakup is not about assigning blame but about gaining clarity. It's an opportunity to reflect on the dynamics of the relationship, the behaviors and patterns that contributed to its demise. Often, breakups are the result of a complex interplay of factors rather than a single event. By dissecting these elements, you can uncover valuable lessons that can guide you in future relationships.

One of the first steps in understanding the breakup is to examine the relationship's foundation. Relationships thrive on a bedrock of mutual respect, trust, and communication. If these fundamental elements were lacking or became compromised, the relationship's stability would inevitably be affected. Reflect on whether there were underlying issues from the beginning. Did you and your partner share the same values and long-term goals? Were there significant differences that were overlooked or minimized in the initial stages? Understanding these foundational aspects can provide insight into the cracks that may have widened over time.

Communication, or the lack thereof, is often a pivotal factor in relationship breakdowns. Consider how you and your partner communicated with each other. Were your conversations open, honest, and respectful, or were they filled with misunderstandings, assumptions, and unresolved conflicts? Effective communication is essential for resolving issues and maintaining a healthy connection. If communication was consistently problematic, it could have created a buildup of unresolved grievances and emotional distance. Reflecting on these patterns can help you identify areas for improvement in future relationships.

Another critical aspect to consider is emotional intimacy. Emotional closeness and vulnerability are the glue that binds partners together. Reflect on whether you and your partner were able to share your true selves. Were you both able to express your fears, dreams, and insecurities without judgment? Emotional intimacy requires trust and a willingness to be vulnerable. If either of you struggled with this, it could have led to feelings of isolation and disconnection. Understanding this aspect can shed light on why the relationship may have faltered.

Healthy relationships involve an equitable distribution of power where both partners feel valued and respected. It's crucial to consider whether there were imbalances in your relationship. Did one partner dominate decision-making, or were both voices heard equally? Were there issues of control, manipulation, or dependency? Recognizing these dynamics is not a sign of weakness, but a step towards empowerment and control. It can help you strive for healthier, more balanced relationships in the future, where you feel more in control and respected. External factors and life circumstances can also play a significant role in the breakdown of a relationship. Consider whether there were external stressors that impacted your relationship. These could include financial difficulties, career pressures, family conflicts, or health issues. Reflecting on how these factors influenced your relationship can provide a broader context for understanding the breakup.

It's also important to examine individual contributions to the relationship's demise. This introspective approach is not about self-blame but about self-awareness and growth. Reflect on your behaviours, attitudes, and reactions. Were there patterns or habits that may have contributed to the relationship's challenges? Did you have unresolved personal issues that impacted your interactions with your partner? Understanding your own role can empower you to make positive changes and avoid repeating the same patterns in future relationships.

Another key aspect to consider is compatibility. While love and attraction are vital, compatibility in values, goals, and lifestyles is equally essential for a lasting relationship. Reflect on whether you and your partner were genuinely compatible. Did you have similar visions for the future? Were your life priorities aligned? Sometimes, despite strong feelings for each other, fundamental differences can create insurmountable obstacles. Recognizing this can help you seek more excellent compatibility in future relationships. The role of unmet needs and expectations is also worth exploring. Every individual has unique needs and expectations in a relationship, and when these are not met, dissatisfaction and frustration can arise. Reflect on whether your needs were acknowledged and fulfilled. Did you feel heard and understood, or were your needs dismissed or minimized? Similarly, consider whether you were able to meet your partner's needs. Understanding these unmet needs can provide clarity on why the relationship struggled and help you articulate and negotiate your needs more effectively in future relationships.

In some cases, breakups occur because individuals grow and change in different directions. Personal growth is a natural and healthy part of life, but sometimes partners evolve in ways that lead them apart rather than together. Reflect on whether there were significant changes in either you or your partner that contributed to the breakup. Did one of you undergo a major life change, such as a career shift, a move, or a personal transformation, that altered the dynamics of the relationship? Understanding these changes can help you appreciate that sometimes, breakups are a result of personal growth rather than failure. Accepting that certain breakups are inevitable and out of your control is crucial, to sum up. Infidelity, abuse, or irreconcilable disagreements might provide insurmountable challenges. In many circumstances, comprehending the breakup entails acknowledging that it was essential for your own well-being and future happiness. While these situations are difficult, they also provide you the opportunity to reclaim your life and go on with more strength and resilience.

When analyzing the reasons behind the breakup, it is critical to approach the process with empathy and self-awareness. Avoid self-blame and harsh criticism. Instead, consider this contemplation a voyage of self-discovery and progress. Understanding the nuances of the relationship and the causes that contributed to its conclusion might provide you with vital insights that will help you form better, more meaningful relationships in the future.

Understanding the breakup is a transformative process that requires honesty, introspection, and a willingness to learn. It's an opportunity to turn pain into wisdom and to emerge from the experience with a deeper understanding of yourself and what you need in a relationship. Embrace this phase with an open heart, knowing that each insight gained brings you closer to healing and a brighter, more empowered future.

Self-reflection is an indispensable tool in the aftermath of a breakup. This introspective process allows you to examine your inner world, your behaviors, and your patterns, providing a clearer understanding of your role in the relationship and its end. Self-reflection is not about assigning blame, either to yourself or your partner, but about gaining insights that foster personal growth and pave the way for healthier future relationships. Start by taking a step back and creating a space for honest self-examination.

This can be a challenging process, as it requires confronting uncomfortable truths and acknowledging areas where you might have fallen short. However, it is through this discomfort that true growth occurs. Begin by reflecting on your behaviors and actions within the relationship. Were there patterns that contributed to conflicts or misunderstandings? Did you communicate your needs effectively, or did you hold back out of fear or insecurity? Understanding these dynamics can illuminate areas for improvement and help you develop healthier communication skills.

Next, consider your emotional responses and triggers. Breakups often highlight unresolved personal issues that can impact relationships. Reflect on whether past experiences or traumas influenced your reactions and interactions with your partner. Were there moments when your responses were disproportionate to the situation? By identifying these triggers, you can work on healing past wounds and developing more balanced emotional responses. This process of self-awareness is crucial for personal growth and lays the foundation for more stable and fulfilling future relationships. Acceptance is a vital part of self-reflection. It involves acknowledging the reality of the breakup and embracing the lessons it offers without clinging to what could have been. Acceptance does not mean condoning any hurtful behavior or minimizing the pain, but rather recognizing the situation as it is and allowing yourself to move forward. This acceptance is a liberating force, freeing you from the shackles of denial and enabling you to focus on healing and growth.

Reflect on the relationship as a whole, considering both the positive and negative aspects. Acknowledge the good times and the love shared, but also recognize the issues and conflicts that led to the breakup. This balanced perspective helps you see the relationship more clearly and understand that it had both strengths and weaknesses. Accepting the relationship in its entirety, rather than idealizing or demonizing it, allows you to learn from the experience and carry those lessons into your future. Closure is another essential element in the healing process, acting as a bridge between the past and the future. It is the process of making peace with the end of the relationship and finding a sense of resolution. Closure can be elusive, especially when breakups are abrupt or surrounded by unresolved issues. However, seeking closure is crucial for emotional healing and moving forward.

One way to seek closure is through open and honest communication with your ex-partner, if possible. This conversation should focus on gaining understanding and expressing your feelings rather than assigning blame or reopening old wounds. It can be helpful to approach this dialogue with a sense of curiosity and a willingness to listen. Understanding your partner's perspective can provide valuable insights and help you see the breakup from a different angle. However, be mindful of your emotional state and whether such a conversation would be beneficial or potentially harmful. When direct communication is not possible or advisable, seeking closure internally becomes even more important. This involves creating your own narrative and finding meaning in the experience. Journaling can be a powerful tool in this process. Write about your feelings, your reflections on the relationship, and what you have learned. Expressing your thoughts on paper can help you process complex emotions and gain clarity. You might also write a letter to your ex-partner, expressing everything you wish you could say, and then decide whether to send it or keep it as a personal exercise.

Rituals and symbolic gestures can also aid in achieving closure. These acts can serve as a physical representation of letting go and moving on. Consider creating a ritual that signifies the end of the relationship and the beginning of a new chapter in your life. This could be as simple as writing down your thoughts and feelings and then burning the paper, symbolizing the release of the past. Alternatively, you might choose to pack away mementos and reminders of the relationship, creating a clear space both physically and emotionally. Forgiveness is a critical component of closure. This does not mean excusing any hurtful behavior but rather releasing the hold that anger and resentment have over you. Holding onto these negative emotions can keep you tethered to the past, hindering your ability to heal and move forward. Forgiving yourself and your ex-partner can be a powerful act of liberation. It allows you to reclaim your power and focus on your own growth and happiness.

Therapy and counseling can also be invaluable in seeking closure and understanding the breakup. A therapist can provide a safe and supportive environment to explore your feelings, gain insights, and develop coping strategies. They can help you navigate complex emotions and provide guidance on finding closure. Additionally, therapy can assist in addressing any underlying issues or patterns that may have contributed to the breakup, fostering long-term personal growth.

Recall that every person's journey toward knowledge and closure is extraordinarily particular and distinct. Finding a path that feels appropriate for you and supports your healing is what is vital in seeking closure; there is no right or wrong way to do it. Have self-compassion and let things happen organically. Closure is a journey, not a destination, and healing takes time.

Chapter Three

Self-Care

In the aftermath of a breakup, the importance of self-care cannot be overstated. This phase of your journey is about rediscovering and nurturing yourself, tending to the wounds of your heart, and rebuilding your strength and resilience. Self-care is not just about physical well-being but also about emotional, mental, and spiritual health. It's a holistic approach to healing that empowers you to move forward with renewed energy and purpose. Navigating self-care during a breakup involves a range of strategies that cater to different aspects of your well-being, helping you reclaim your life and find joy again.

One of the first steps in self-care is to prioritize your physical health. The emotional toll of a breakup can often manifest physically, leading to fatigue, sleep disturbances, and changes in appetite. Taking care of your body is a foundational aspect of healing. Start by establishing a routine that includes regular exercise. Physical activity releases endorphins, which are natural mood lifters. Whether it's a brisk walk, yoga, or a more intense workout, find an activity that you enjoy and make it a part of your daily routine. Exercise not only boosts your mood but also helps you manage stress and anxiety.

A healthy diet is essential to your overall health. It's simple to ignore good eating practices when under stress, either by overeating or losing your appetite. Prioritize eating a well-balanced diet that includes whole grains, lean meats, fruits, and vegetables. These foods supply vital nutrients that help your body repair and rejuvenate. Drink lots of water to stay hydrated, and cut back on alcohol and coffee as these substances can worsen anxiety and interfere with sleep. Sleep is another critical component of physical self-care. Breakups can wreak havoc on your sleep patterns, leading to insomnia or restless nights. Establish a calming bedtime routine to signal to your body that it's time to wind down. This might include activities like reading, taking a warm bath, or practising relaxation techniques such as deep breathing or meditation. Aim for a consistent sleep schedule, going to bed and waking up at the same time each day. Quality sleep is essential for emotional regulation, cognitive function, and overall resilience. Emotional self-care is equally vital in the wake of a breakup. Allow yourself to feel and process your emotions without judgment. It's natural to experience a wide range of feelings, from sadness and anger to relief and confusion. Journaling can be a powerful tool for emotional self-care. Writing about your thoughts and feelings helps you process complex emotions and gain clarity. It provides a safe space to express yourself freely and reflect on your experiences.

Surrounding yourself with supportive people is another key aspect of emotional self-care. Reach out to friends and family who can offer a listening ear, comfort, and encouragement. Talking about your feelings with someone you trust can provide relief and perspective. If you find it challenging to open up to those close to you, consider seeking support from a therapist or counselor. Professional guidance can help you navigate your emotions and develop coping strategies tailored to your needs.

Engaging in activities that bring you joy and relaxation is an important part of emotional self-care. Rediscover hobbies and interests that you may have neglected during the relationship. Whether it's painting, gardening, cooking, or playing a musical instrument, immerse yourself in activities that make you happy. These moments of joy and creativity provide a much-needed respite from the emotional turmoil and help you reconnect with yourself. Mental self-care involves nurturing your mind and maintaining a positive outlook. Breakups can often lead to negative thought patterns and self-doubt. Practicing mindfulness and meditation can help you stay grounded and present. These practices encourage you to observe your thoughts without judgment and reduce the impact of negative thinking. Even a few minutes of mindfulness each day can make a significant difference in your mental well-being.

Setting boundaries is another important aspect of mental self-care. In the aftermath of a breakup, it's crucial to protect your emotional space. This might mean limiting contact with your ex-partner, at least temporarily, to give yourself time to heal. It could also involve setting boundaries with friends or family members who may have strong opinions about your breakup. Communicate your needs clearly and prioritize your well-being. Boundaries help you maintain control over your emotional landscape and create a safe environment for healing.

Spiritual self-care is about connecting with something greater than yourself, whether it's through religion, nature, or personal spirituality. This connection can provide a sense of peace and purpose during difficult times. Engage in practices that nourish your spirit, such as prayer, meditation, or spending time in nature. Reflect on your values and beliefs, and seek meaning and inspiration from them. Spiritual self-care helps you find inner strength and resilience, guiding you through the healing process.

Self-compassion is a cornerstone of self-care. Treat yourself with the same kindness and understanding that you would offer a friend going through a difficult time. Acknowledge your pain and struggles without self-criticism. Practice positive self-talk, reminding yourself of your strengths and worth. Self-compassion fosters a supportive inner dialogue and helps you build a positive relationship with yourself. Creating a self-care plan can provide structure and focus during this challenging time. Start by identifying the areas of self-care that resonate most with you, whether physical, emotional, mental, or spiritual. Set realistic goals and incorporate self-care activities into your daily routine. This plan can serve as a guide, reminding you to prioritize your well-being and stay committed to your healing journey.

Self-care is not a one-size-fits-all approach. It's about finding what works best for you and being flexible as your needs evolve. Some days, you might need more rest and solitude, while other days, you might seek connection and activity. Listen to your body and mind, and honor what you need in each moment. Remember that self-care is a continuous practice, not a destination. It's an ongoing commitment to nurturing yourself and fostering resilience. As you navigate self-care during a breakup, remind yourself that healing is a journey, not a race. Be patient with yourself and celebrate small victories along the way. Each act of self-care, no matter how small, contributes to your overall well-being and recovery. By prioritizing self-care, you are investing in your future happiness and creating a solid foundation for personal growth and resilience.

Self-care is not a one-size-fits-all approach. It's about finding what works best for you and being flexible as your needs evolve. Some days, you might need more rest and solitude, while other days, you might seek connection and activity. Listen to your body and mind, and honor what you need in each moment. Remember that self-care is a continuous practice, not a destination. It's an ongoing commitment to nurturing yourself and fostering resilience.

Physical Well-Being:

- **Exercise Regularly:** Engage in physical activities you enjoy, whether it's a brisk walk, yoga, or a more intense workout. Aim for at least 30 minutes of exercise most days of the week to boost your mood and manage stress.

- **Eat Nutritious Foods:** Focus on a balanced diet rich in fruits, vegetables, lean proteins, and whole grains. Stay hydrated by drinking plenty of water and limit alcohol and caffeine intake.

- **Establish a Sleep Routine:** Create a calming bedtime routine and aim for a consistent sleep schedule. Practices like reading, taking a warm bath, or deep breathing can help signal your body that it's time to wind down.

Emotional Well-Being:

- **Allow Yourself to Feel:** Give yourself permission to experience a range of emotions without judgment. Journaling can help you process these emotions and gain clarity.

- **Seek Support:** Surround yourself with supportive friends and family. If needed, consider professional counseling to navigate complex emotions and develop coping strategies.

- **Engage in Joyful Activities:** Rediscover hobbies and interests that bring you happiness. Whether it's painting, gardening, or cooking, immerse yourself in activities that provide a sense of joy and relaxation.

Mental Well-Being:

- **Practice Mindfulness:** Incorporate mindfulness and meditation into your routine. Even a few minutes each day can help you stay grounded and reduce the impact of negative thoughts.

- **Set Boundaries:** Protect your emotional space by setting boundaries with your ex-partner and others who may have strong opinions about your breakup. Communicate your needs clearly and prioritize your well-being.

- **Focus on Positive Self-Talk:** Cultivate a supportive inner dialogue. Practice positive affirmations and remind yourself of your strengths and worth.

Spiritual Well-Being:

- **Connect with Your Spirituality:** Engage in practices that nourish your spirit, such as prayer, meditation, or spending time in nature. Reflect on your values and beliefs, and seek meaning and inspiration from them.

- **Practice Self-Compassion:** Treat yourself with the same kindness and understanding that you would offer a friend. Acknowledge your pain and struggles without self-criticism.

Creating a comprehensive self-care plan that includes these practical tips and exercises can help you navigate the healing process more effectively. Self-care is a continuous practice that evolves with your needs, providing a solid foundation for personal growth and resilience. Embrace this journey with an open heart, knowing that each step brings you closer to healing and renewal.

Chapter Four

Rediscovering your Identity

Rediscovering your identity after a breakup presents a crucial step in your healing journey. Breakups often leave us feeling disconnected from ourselves, our sense of self intertwined with the relationship that has ended. Reclaiming your identity involves peeling away the layers of who you became within the relationship and reconnecting with your core self. The first step in this process involves spending time alone.

Solitude may seem daunting, especially when you have grown accustomed to constant companionship. Embrace this solitude as an opportunity to listen to your inner voice. Spend quiet moments reflecting on your thoughts, desires, and aspirations. Meditation or quiet walks can help facilitate this introspection, allowing you to tune into your innermost self.

Next, revisit your passions and hobbies. During a relationship, you may have sidelined activities that once brought you joy. Rekindle these interests. If you loved painting, pick up a brush again. If you enjoyed hiking, lace up your boots and hit the trails. Engaging in activities you love reminds you of your unique interests and reaffirms your individuality. Setting personal goals also plays a vital role in rediscovering your identity. Reflect on areas of your life you want to develop or change. Perhaps you wish to advance in your career, learn a new skill, or travel. Set realistic, achievable goals and create a plan to reach them. Pursuing these goals provides direction and purpose, helping you focus on your growth and development.

Connecting with new people and expanding your social circle can also aid in rediscovering your identity. Meet people who share your interests and values. Join clubs, attend workshops, or participate in community events. These new interactions can offer fresh perspectives and inspire personal growth, enriching your understanding of yourself and your place in the world.

Journaling serves as another powerful tool for self-discovery. Write about your thoughts, feelings, and experiences regularly. Reflect on what you learn about yourself through these writings. Journaling helps you process your emotions and gain clarity on your identity, providing a tangible record of your growth and evolution. Embrace the changes you experience.

Breakups often lead to significant personal transformation. Accept these changes as part of your journey. Allow yourself to evolve and grow. Change can feel unsettling, but it also brings opportunities for self-discovery and renewal. Embrace this transformation with an open heart, ready to learn and grow. Cultivating self-compassion stands as a cornerstone of rediscovering your identity. Treat yourself with kindness and understanding, acknowledging your efforts and progress. Celebrate your achievements, no matter how small. Self-compassion fosters a positive relationship with yourself, empowering you to embrace your true identity.

Explore your values and beliefs. Reflect on what matters most to you. What principles guide your actions? What do you stand for? Understanding your core values helps you align your actions with your true self, reinforcing your identity. This alignment brings a sense of authenticity and integrity to your life.

Seek out new experiences. Travel to new places, try different activities, or take up a new hobby. These experiences challenge you and push you out of your comfort zone, revealing aspects of yourself you may not have known. Embrace these opportunities for growth and self-discovery.

Lastly, remember that rediscovering your identity takes time. Be patient with yourself. This journey is not a race but a continuous process of self-exploration and growth. Allow yourself the time and space to fully engage in this process, knowing that each step brings you closer to a deeper understanding of yourself.

Self-Discovery and Personal Growth Opportunities

Rediscovering your identity after a breakup naturally opens the door to self-discovery and personal growth. This phase marks a time of profound transformation where you can explore new dimensions of yourself, unearthing talents, strengths, and passions that may have been dormant. Embrace this journey not merely as a recovery process but as an opportunity to blossom into a more self-aware and resilient individual. The process of self-discovery begins with introspection. Take the time to ask yourself probing questions about your desires, aspirations, and fears. What do you truly want out of life? What are your passions and interests? What beliefs and values do you hold dear? Reflecting on these questions helps you gain a deeper understanding of who you are and what you stand for, laying the foundation for personal growth.

Personal growth opportunities often arise when you step out of your comfort zone. Challenge yourself to try new activities or learn new skills. This might involve enrolling in a course, picking up a new hobby, or pursuing a career change. Each new experience broadens your horizons and exposes you to different perspectives, contributing to your personal development. Embrace these challenges as they push you to adapt and grow, building your resilience and self-confidence.

Another vital aspect of self-discovery is recognizing and embracing your strengths and weaknesses. Understanding your capabilities allows you to leverage your strengths to achieve your goals, while acknowledging your weaknesses provides a path for improvement. Use this awareness to set realistic, attainable goals that align with your values and aspirations. Each goal you achieve, no matter how small, builds your self-esteem and propels you further on your growth journey. Engage in continuous learning. Whether through formal education, self-study, or experiential learning, expanding your knowledge enriches your mind and opens up new possibilities. Read widely, attend seminars, or engage in discussions that challenge your thinking. Knowledge empowers you, enhancing your understanding of the world and your place within it, and fostering personal growth.

Building emotional intelligence represents another significant opportunity for personal growth. Emotional intelligence involves understanding and managing your emotions, as well as recognizing and empathizing with the emotions of others. Developing this skill helps you navigate relationships more effectively and enhances your ability to cope with stress and adversity. Practice mindfulness and self-awareness to improve your emotional intelligence, leading to healthier interactions and a more balanced emotional state. Explore and nurture your creativity. Creativity is not limited to the arts; it encompasses any activity that allows you to express yourself and think outside the box. Whether it's writing, painting, cooking, or problem-solving, engaging in creative pursuits stimulates your mind and enhances your ability to innovate. Creativity also provides an outlet for processing emotions and can be deeply therapeutic, aiding in your healing and growth.

Volunteering and helping others can also be a powerful avenue for self-discovery and growth. Giving your time and skills to a cause you care about not only benefits the community but also fosters a sense of purpose and fulfillment. Volunteering allows you to connect with others, develop new skills, and gain perspective on your own life. It reinforces your values and can reveal aspects of your character you might not have recognized. Practicing gratitude and positive thinking plays a crucial role in personal growth. Cultivating a mindset of gratitude shifts your focus from what you lack to what you have, fostering a sense of contentment and appreciation. Regularly reflecting on things you are grateful for enhances your overall well-being and resilience. Positive thinking helps you overcome obstacles and maintain a hopeful outlook, propelling you forward on your growth journey.

Self-discovery and personal growth also involve embracing change and uncertainty. Life is inherently unpredictable, and learning to navigate its twists and turns with flexibility and grace is a mark of personal growth. Embrace the changes that come your way, viewing them as opportunities for learning and development. Each challenge you overcome strengthens your resilience and prepares you for future obstacles. Building and maintaining healthy relationships contributes to personal growth. Surround yourself with supportive, positive individuals who encourage your development. Engage in meaningful conversations and activities that enrich your life. Healthy relationships provide a safe space for self-expression and growth, offering support and encouragement as you navigate your journey of self-discovery.

Lastly, practice self-compassion throughout your journey. Be patient and kind to yourself as you explore new facets of your identity and strive for personal growth. Acknowledge your efforts and celebrate your achievements, no matter how small. Self-compassion fosters a positive relationship with yourself, essential for sustained growth and well-being.

Chapter Five

Building a Support System

During the recovery process after a breakup, building and maintaining a support system is essential for emotional healing and resilience. A support system consists of individuals who offer understanding, encouragement, and practical assistance during challenging times. These relationships play a crucial role in providing emotional validation, perspective, and a sense of belonging, all of which contribute to your overall well-being and recovery.

One of the primary benefits of a support system is emotional validation. Breakups often evoke intense emotions such as sadness, anger, and loneliness. Having supportive friends, family members, or even a therapist who listen without judgment and validate your feelings can be immensely comforting. They reassure you that your emotions are valid and understandable, helping you process and navigate through them. Perspective is another invaluable aspect provided by a support system. When you're immersed in the emotional turmoil of a breakup, it's easy to lose sight of the bigger picture. Supportive individuals can offer objective viewpoints and alternative perspectives, helping you see beyond immediate pain and envision a future beyond the breakup. Their insights can broaden your understanding of the situation and provide clarity during moments of confusion.

A support system fosters a sense of belonging and connection. Breakups can leave you feeling isolated and adrift. Building a support network of trusted individuals creates a sense of community and belonging. Knowing that you are not alone in your struggles and that others care about your well-being strengthens your resilience. It reinforces your sense of identity and self-worth, reminding you that you are valued and appreciated despite the challenges you face.

Practical assistance is also a vital component of a support system. Friends and family members can offer tangible support such as helping with daily tasks, providing a listening ear, or offering financial assistance if needed. Practical support alleviates stress and allows you to focus on your emotional recovery. It may involve simple gestures like preparing a meal, running errands, or providing childcare, all of which contribute to your overall well-being during a difficult time. Support networks provide encouragement and motivation to move forward. Breakups can diminish self-confidence and create doubts about the future. Supportive individuals offer words of encouragement, affirming your strengths and capabilities. Their belief in your resilience and potential inspires you to take steps toward healing and rebuilding your life. Encouragement from others can ignite hope and optimism, empowering you to embrace new opportunities and challenges.

Building a support system involves both reaching out to others and being open to receiving support. Initiate conversations with trusted individuals about your feelings and experiences. Share your needs and allow others to offer their support in ways that are meaningful to you. Cultivate relationships built on trust, empathy, and mutual respect. A strong support system is characterized by reciprocity, where both parties give and receive support when needed. Identify individuals in your life who have demonstrated empathy, reliability, and a genuine concern for your well-being.

These qualities indicate their capacity to provide meaningful support during your recovery. Consider seeking professional support from a therapist or counselor trained in helping individuals navigate through the emotional challenges of a breakup. Professional guidance can offer specialized insights and coping strategies tailored to your unique situation.

- ➤ **Friends:** Friends often play a pivotal role in providing emotional support during a breakup. They offer empathy, companionship, and a listening ear. Friends can validate your feelings, share their own experiences, and offer perspective from outside the relationship. They provide a sense of camaraderie and understanding, reminding you that you are not alone in your struggles. Friends may also engage in activities with you, providing distractions and opportunities for enjoyment.

- ➤ **Family:** Family members can offer unconditional love, support, and stability during challenging times. They have a deeper understanding of your history and values, which can provide comfort and reassurance. Family support may involve practical assistance, such as helping with household tasks, providing financial support, or offering childcare. Family members can also offer wisdom and guidance based on their life experiences, helping you navigate through difficult emotions and decisions.

➢ **Therapy:** Therapy or counseling provides professional support from trained therapists or counselors who specialize in helping individuals navigate through emotional challenges, including breakups. Therapists offer a safe and confidential space to explore your feelings, gain insight into patterns of behavior, and develop coping strategies. Therapy can help you process grief, manage stress, improve communication skills, and rebuild self-esteem. Therapists use evidence-based techniques to address specific issues and provide personalized guidance tailored to your needs.

1. **Recognize the Need for Support:** Acknowledge your emotional needs and recognize when additional support is beneficial. Common signs that you may benefit from support include feeling overwhelmed by emotions, difficulty functioning in daily life, persistent sadness or anxiety, and challenges in coping with the breakup. Seeking support is a proactive step toward healing and rebuilding your life.

2. **Identify Trusted Individuals:** Identify friends and family members who demonstrate empathy, reliability, and a genuine concern for your well-being. These individuals are more likely to offer meaningful support during your recovery. Consider reaching out to those who have

supported you in the past or who have experience navigating similar challenges.

3. **Communicate Your Needs:** Be open and honest about your feelings and needs when seeking support. Clearly communicate how others can support you, whether it's through listening without judgment, offering practical assistance, or simply spending time together. Expressing your needs helps others understand how they can best support you during this time.

4. **Be Open to Different Forms of Support:** Recognize that support can come in various forms, and different types of support may be beneficial at different stages of your recovery. For example, while friends may provide emotional validation and companionship, therapy can offer specialized guidance and tools for emotional healing and personal growth. Be

open to exploring different avenues of support to find what works best for you.

5. **Seek Professional Help When Needed:** Consider seeking professional help from a therapist or counselor if you find it challenging to cope with intense emotions or if your recovery is hindered by persistent distress. Therapists are trained to provide objective support and specialized interventions that promote healing and resilience. Therapy offers a structured approach to addressing emotional challenges and developing effective coping strategies.

6. **Practice Self-Compassion:** Be kind and patient with yourself as you seek and accept help. Recognize that seeking support is a sign of strength, not weakness. Allow yourself to receive support without feeling guilty or ashamed. Embrace self-

compassion by treating yourself with the same understanding and care that you would offer a friend in need.

7. **Set Boundaries:** Maintain boundaries within your support network to protect your emotional well-being. Clearly communicate your limits and preferences regarding the type and frequency of support you need. Respect the boundaries of others within your support system as well. Healthy relationships are built on mutual respect and understanding of each other's needs.

Chapter Six

Letting Go and Forgiveness

Letting go of resentment and anger after a breakup is a profound process of emotional liberation and healing. Resentment and anger are natural responses to hurt and betrayal, but holding onto these emotions can prolong your pain and hinder your ability to move forward. The process of letting go begins with acknowledging and validating your feelings without judgment. Allow yourself to experience the anger and resentment you may be feeling fully. Understand that these emotions are valid reactions to the pain you have experienced.

To facilitate letting go, it is essential to cultivate self-awareness and insight into the underlying causes of your anger and resentment. Reflect on how these emotions manifest in your thoughts, behaviors, and relationships. Identify the beliefs and expectations that contribute to your feelings of resentment. Often, these beliefs are rooted in a sense of injustice or betrayal, where you feel wronged or unfairly treated. By understanding the origins of your emotions, you can begin to challenge and reframe these beliefs, opening the path to forgiveness.

Forgiveness is a powerful antidote to resentment and anger. It is not about condoning or excusing the actions of others but releasing yourself from the emotional burden of holding onto negative feelings. Forgiveness is a conscious decision to let go of resentment and replace it with compassion and understanding. It involves accepting the reality of what happened and choosing to free yourself from the emotional ties that bind you to the past. Forgiveness allows you to reclaim your power and emotional well-being, moving from victimhood to empowerment. Forgiveness also extends to oneself. It is expected to harbor guilt, shame, or self-blame after a breakup, questioning decisions made or actions taken. Self-forgiveness involves accepting your imperfections and mistakes with compassion and understanding. It is about recognizing that you did the best you could with the knowledge and resources available to you at the time. Self-forgiveness allows you to release self-judgment and embrace self-compassion, fostering a more profound sense of self-acceptance and inner peace.

Practicing forgiveness requires intentional effort and commitment. Begin by acknowledging the hurt and pain caused by the breakup. Allow yourself to grieve the loss of the relationship and the future you had envisioned. Journaling can be a helpful tool for processing emotions and gaining clarity on your feelings. Write about your experiences, thoughts, and reflections on forgiveness. Expressing your feelings through writing can provide a sense of release and facilitate healing.

Reflect on the broader implications of forgiveness in your life. Consider how holding onto resentment and anger impacts your relationships, health, and overall well-being. Recognize that forgiveness is a gift you give yourself, not to the person who hurt you. It liberates you from the past and empowers you to create a future filled with peace and emotional freedom. Visualize yourself letting go of resentment and embracing forgiveness as a transformative process of healing and growth.

Practice empathy and compassion toward the person who hurt you. Understand that everyone has their own struggles, insecurities, and limitations. Recognize the humanity in others, acknowledging that they too are flawed and imperfect. Empathy does not require you to condone their actions but allows you to see beyond their behaviors to the deeper motivations and emotions driving their actions. Cultivating empathy can soften feelings of resentment and foster a sense of connection and understanding. Forgiveness exercises can aid in the forgiveness process. Practice writing a forgiveness letter, expressing your feelings and intentions without expecting a response. Alternatively, practice visualization exercises where you imagine releasing negative emotions and replacing them with feelings of peace and acceptance. Engage in forgiveness meditations or guided imagery exercises that focus on letting go of resentment and cultivating compassion. These exercises encourage introspection and facilitate emotional healing.

In conclusion, letting go of resentment and anger through forgiveness is a transformative process of emotional liberation and healing. It involves acknowledging and validating your feelings, cultivating self-awareness and insight, and making a conscious decision to release negative emotions. Forgiveness extends to both others and oneself, allowing you to reclaim your power and emotional well-being. By practicing empathy, compassion, and forgiveness exercises, you can facilitate the forgiveness process and pave the way for healing, inner peace, and personal growth.

Chapter Seven

Embracing Change and New Beginnings

Embracing change after a breakup is often a daunting but essential part of the healing process. Change signifies the end of one chapter and the beginning of another a period ripe with opportunities for personal growth, self-discovery, and new beginnings. Rather than fearing or resisting change, embracing it as a catalyst for transformation can empower you to navigate through this transition with resilience and optimism.

Change offers an opportunity for growth by challenging you to step outside your comfort zone and explore new possibilities. It encourages self-reflection and introspection, prompting you to reassess your values, priorities, and aspirations. Embracing change involves adopting a growth mindset, a belief that challenges and setbacks are opportunities for learning and development. This mindset fosters resilience, adaptability, and a willingness to embrace uncertainty as part of the journey toward personal fulfillment. Setting new goals and aspirations is a pivotal step in embracing change and creating a future aligned with your evolving desires. Begin by reflecting on your passions, interests, and values. What activities or experiences bring you joy and fulfillment? What long-term goals or dreams have you postponed or set aside? Setting meaningful goals provides direction and purpose, motivating you to take proactive steps toward achieving your aspirations.

When setting goals, prioritize clarity, specificity, and feasibility. Define clear objectives that align with your values and aspirations. Break larger goals into smaller, manageable tasks to maintain momentum and track progress. Celebrate each achievement, no matter how small, as a step forward on your journey. Goal-setting empowers you to take control of your future and actively shape the life you envision beyond the confines of your past relationship.

Moving forward with positivity and hope involves cultivating a mindset of optimism and resilience. Acknowledge and honor your emotions, allowing yourself to grieve the loss of the relationship and the future you had envisioned. Practice self-compassion by treating yourself with kindness and understanding during moments of self-doubt or difficulty. Surround yourself with supportive individuals who encourage your growth and uplift your spirits.

Focus on the present moment and embrace opportunities for self-care and personal enrichment. Engage in activities that nurture your physical, emotional, and mental well-being, such as exercise, meditation, creative pursuits, or spending time in nature. Prioritize activities that bring you joy and foster a sense of fulfillment. Cultivate gratitude by reflecting on the positive aspects of your life and expressing appreciation for the support and opportunities available to you.

Seek inspiration from role models or individuals who have navigated through similar challenges and emerged stronger and more resilient. Their stories of perseverance and triumph can provide encouragement and guidance as you embark on your own journey of personal growth and transformation. Draw strength from their experiences and insights, knowing that you too have the inner resources to overcome adversity and create a fulfilling life.

Embracing change also involves letting go of limiting beliefs or self-imposed barriers that may hinder your progress. Challenge negative self-talk and replace it with affirmations of self-worth and empowerment. Recognize that change is a natural and inevitable part of life, offering opportunities for renewal and reinvention. Embrace uncertainty as a source of potential and possibility, rather than fear or apprehension.

Practice resilience by adapting to challenges and setbacks with grace and determination. View obstacles as opportunities for learning and growth, reframing setbacks as temporary setbacks on your path to success. Cultivate flexibility and openness to new experiences, recognizing that each experience whether positive or challenging contributes to your personal growth and development.

Celebrate your progress and achievements along the way, acknowledging the courage and resilience it takes to embrace change and pursue new beginnings. Recognize that growth is a continuous journey, marked by self-discovery, learning, and adaptation. Embrace change as an opportunity to create a life that reflects your values, passions, and aspirations a life filled with purpose, fulfillment, and meaningful connections.

In conclusion, embracing change and new beginnings after a breakup involves adopting a growth mindset, setting new goals and aspirations, and moving forward with positivity and hope. By embracing change as a catalyst for personal growth, setting clear and meaningful goals, cultivating resilience and optimism, and letting go of limiting beliefs, you can navigate through this transition with confidence and grace.

Embrace the opportunities for self-discovery, learning, and transformation that change brings, knowing that each step forward brings you closer to a life of fulfillment and possibility.

Chapter Eight

Thriving in Your New Life

Thriving in your new life after a breakup encompasses integrating key lessons and insights gained from your recovery journey, maintaining emotional resilience, and embracing life with a renewed sense of purpose and joy. As you reflect on your experiences and growth, recognize that each challenge you faced has contributed to your resilience and personal development. Here, we summarize the essential lessons and insights, explore strategies for sustaining emotional well-being, and encourage you to celebrate the journey that has led you to this transformative moment. Reflecting on your recovery journey reveals valuable lessons and insights that have shaped your personal growth. Recognize the strength and resilience you have cultivated through adversity. Acknowledge the importance of self-care and self-compassion in nurturing your emotional well-being. Understand the transformative power of forgiveness, both for yourself and others, in releasing the emotional burdens of the past. Embrace change as an opportunity for growth and renewal, fostering a mindset of optimism and possibility. Celebrate the relationships and support systems that have uplifted and guided you through difficult times. These lessons serve as guiding principles as you navigate your new life with courage and conviction.

Maintaining emotional resilience is essential for navigating life's challenges with grace and resilience. Practice mindfulness and self-awareness to stay attuned to your emotions and thoughts. Engage in regular self-care practices that nurture your physical, emotional, and mental well-being, such as exercise, meditation, and creative pursuits. Cultivate a strong support network of friends, family, or community members who provide encouragement, empathy, and practical assistance. Set realistic goals and priorities that align with your values and aspirations, allowing you to focus your energy on meaningful endeavors. Develop healthy coping strategies for managing stress and adversity, such as positive self-talk, relaxation techniques, or seeking professional support when needed. By fostering emotional resilience, you empower yourself to face life's challenges with resilience and optimism.

Embrace life fully by embracing opportunities for growth, connection, and fulfillment. Embrace your passions and interests, pursuing activities that bring you joy and purpose. Cultivate meaningful relationships that nurture your spirit and enhance your sense of belonging. Celebrate your achievements and milestones, no matter how small, as they reflect your perseverance and determination.

Practice gratitude for the abundance and blessings in your life, fostering a sense of contentment and appreciation. Embrace new experiences and challenges with openness and enthusiasm, knowing that each moment offers an opportunity for learning and personal growth. By celebrating your journey and embracing life fully, you create a life of meaning, resilience, and joy.

THE END